Meanwhile / *Take My Hand*

Meanwhile / *Take My Hand*

Kirmen Uribe /

TRANSLATED FROM
THE BASQUE BY
Elizabeth Macklin

Graywolf Press
Saint Paul, Minnesota

Publication of this volume is made possible in part by a grant provided by the
Minnesota State Arts Board, through an appropriation by the Minnesota State
Legislature; a grant from the Wells Fargo Foundation Minnesota; and a grant
from the National Endowment for the Arts, which believes that a great nation
deserves great art. Significant support has also been provided by the Bush
Foundation; Target; the McKnight Foundation; and other generous contributions
from foundations, corporations, and individuals. To these organizations and
individuals we offer our heartfelt thanks.

A Lannan Translation Selection
Funding the translation and publication of exceptional literary works

Published by Graywolf Press
2402 University Avenue, Suite 203
Saint Paul, Minnesota 55114
All rights reserved.

www.graywolfpress.org

Published in the United States of America

ISBN-13 978-1-55597-458-9
ISBN-10 1-55597-458-9
2 4 6 8 9 7 5 3 1
First Graywolf Printing, 2007

Library of Congress Control Number: 2006924342

Cover design: Kyle G. Hunter

Cover photograph: © Es/Veer

Acknowledgments

Thanks to the editors of the following magazines, in which these translations first appeared:

Arson: "Cardiogram," "The Aresti-Duchamp Chess Game"
Bloom: "Danger," "Apples"
Circumference: "The Island," "No Saying," "The Cuckoo"
Hogtown Creek Review: "Notes on a Loose Piece of Paper"
The New Yorker: "May"
Open City: "The River," "Visit"
Pequod: "The Space-Time of Trees," "Gadda"
Rattapallax: "I Love You, No," "Birds in Winter," "The Gold Ring"
Southwest Review: "The Cherry Tree," "There's a Fear"
St. Ann's Review: "Postwar," "Bad Dream," "The Fishbowl"
Washington Square: "After John Keats's Gravestone," "Way Off There"

"I Love You, No," "Things That Are Perfect," "The Gold Ring," "Don't Make It a Choice," "The Cuckoo," and "Notes on a Loose Piece of Paper" first appeared in the CD-book *Zaharregia, txikiegia agian / Una manera de mirar / Too Old, Too Small, Maybe* (Paper Hotsak; 2003), in earlier versions, and are reprinted here with gratitude.

Thanks to the editors of *Circumference* for including "The Cuckoo" in their Homophonic Feature; to Lyrikline.org for posting an earlier version of "Birds in Winter" on their spoken-word web site; and especially to the English Centre of International PEN, for reprinting "Don't Make It a Choice" on their web site's Writers in Translation page.

My most heartfelt thanks to the Amy Lowell Poetry Traveling Scholarship Committee and to PEN American Center's Translation Fund, for the wherewithal to begin and to complete this collection.

Contents

Introduction

Kirmen Uribe was born in 1970, in Ondarroa, a fishing town on the Bay of Biscay whose port and canneries now handle much of the catch between Galicia and Bayonne on Spain's northern coast. His father, who died in 1999, and four of his uncles were trawlermen out of Ondarroa and brought their catch back to a long, broad expanse of macadam beside the moorings. In the afternoons the fish pier is still busy with trucks loading shallow crates of anchovies, bonito, and hake, cod, sole, and Norwegian lobster off returning boats.

Ondarroa (accent on the first "a") is built into a rough cup in steep, gray cliffs, with harbor and seawalled port spread out across its bottom, along with two small sand beaches, all occupying just under a square mile and a half. From the port all streets rise and, as they move inland, get older; the immense church that hovers amid the upper townscape was built in the thirteenth century. When you turn and face north, from the fish pier a good half of the seascape is blocked from sight behind the high seawall, which juts from the bottom of a taller headland to the west. To the northeast, there's a clear view out to open sea, almost to France. More easterly still, cliffs block the view again, hiding any trace of Mutriku, the next town over. In the middle distance, though, you can see Ondarroa's small, half-moon beach and, beyond it and an outcrop green with scrub trees, another half-moon beach, called Saturraran.

I first learned the name "Saturraran" from two pieces of Kirmen Uribe's. One, called "Notes on Perception," quoted from a collection of letters written by women who, during the decade of reprisal justice that followed the Spanish Civil War, were kept in a prison that had stood on the beach, a commandeered seminary. In the letter he cites, a woman tells her sister of arriving there by night, with her small daughter, "entirely calm," and only the next morning waking to the truth of where they'd ended up, as she sees by daylight the "wasted, lost faces" around them.

In the other piece, a kind of memory exercise called "Saturraran," Uribe is walking on the beach with his mother, long after the prison building has been razed, when they see a woman, of about his mother's age, who, with her husband, has come to visit the place. Watching her from a distance, they understand the woman to have been one of the children who were imprisoned in Saturraran. His mother looks out at the waves for a long moment, then says to him: "Look, that wave has gone forever." He suddenly finds that whatever he'd been about to say to her has gone right out of his mind.

/

Ondarroa is home to some 9,900 people now, down from about 14,000 when Uribe was growing up. Just one of his cousins goes out on the fishing boats. Uribe's mother lives in a farmhouse set back from the cliff that overhangs Saturraran, and these last months he has been living there, writing in a room that looks out at the ocean. He moved back after eighteen years away. "Because of the obvious difficulties the topography poses in gaining access to towns inland," Ondarroa's web site says, "the town offers everything," and Uribe has said something similar, though he does go to Bilbao, the provincial capital, nearly every week. Except for a half-dozen cousins or so, his remaining family in Ondarroa are all of his parents' generation and older.

People in Ondarroa speak a variant, thick and intact, of Vizcayan, one of seven dialects in Euskara, as Basque is called by the six or seven hundred thousand people who speak it. In Ondarroa a *tripitrapu* is a hopping creature that can be either a toad or a frog. In Lekeitio, the next town to the west, just ten miles away, the same kind of creature is an *ugaraixua* (an *x* is a *sh* sound in Basque). In Euskara Batua, or Unified Basque, a standardized amalgam of dialects that was doggedly cobbled together in the 1960s and is now taught in the schools, "frog" is *igela*, and "toad" is *apoa*, or *zapua*, or *txantxikoa*.

In "The Language of the Animals" Uribe opted for Ondarroa's *tripi-trapu*. But in a schoolroom once, speaking to adults in an intermediate Basque class, he didn't think twice before he answered one of the questions. "If Vizcayan is your own dialect, how come you write in Batua?" a student asked. His immediate answer: "So people will understand me."

/

Uribe, who was five when Francisco Franco died and eight when Spain got its present Constitution, is a member of the first generation of Basques able to start school in their own language. He is also one of a number of people his age, throughout the Peninsula, who have been trying to understand, or to imagine, their grandparents' experience—that of the generation who lived (or died) as adults during and after the Spanish Civil War. From the present of the twenty-first century, it can be a leap of imagination even back to the experience of their parents, who grew up during the dictatorship's so-called Forty Years of Peace and Victory. This new generation, along with a number of their elders, has been digging for documents for clues to how and where wartime and postwar reprisals took place; engaging in forensic archeology (as the Association for the Recovery of Historical Memory has been doing); and, especially in the arts, charting the war's tricklings-down into the present. In any event, the childhood friend in Uribe's poem "Danger," who "picked up bombs bare-handed," found them right where they'd been left, whenever that particular front of the war was lost.

/

From Ondarroa, it's about an hour by bus to Bilbao, on two-lane roads up out of the basin of the Artibai estuary, past cliffs and steeply tilted green sheep meadows to the *autopista* and from there (in twenty or thirty minutes) to the city of Bilbao (pop. around 400,000), on the fourth estuary to the west. Uribe first moved to Bilbao for a year in 1988, when it was still a purely industrial city, to start at the university there. He would return to Greater Bilbao for twelve months in 1995, to go to jail. Uribe was a conscientious objector before Spain abolished, in 1996, the leftover-from-Franco *mili*—universal compulsory military service. When he turned eighteen and his number came up (as every young man's did), he joined the Peninsula-wide anti-militarist and pacifist movement called *insumismo* (in Basque, *intsumisioa*), which had emerged, in the mid-1980s, in conjunction with the widespread outcry against Spain's joining NATO. If you've already had a war you sure don't need to be anywhere near another one, was the thought. *Insumismo* encouraged principled draft resistance, and Spain offered no provision for conscientious objectors except a one- to two-year jail term. An anecdote Uribe tells as a funny story has to do with accepting his first literary prize (for a book-length essay) in handcuffs. By 1995, when he was doing his time, many other young men—by the hundreds, he says—were serving sentences for *intsumisioa* with him in Basauri prison, just over the city line.

In 1989, Uribe moved to Vitoria-Gasteiz, the regional capital, about half the size of Bilbao, to begin a Basque-philology major at the university there. He lived not far from the Basque-speaking enclave on Kutxi—Calle Cuchillería, one of the medieval Old Quarter streets that form a Christ Pantocrator's almond shape as they climb the city's hill. You could always find a way to pass some time in the funky taverns lining Kutxi. There was always someone around: a friend, an acquaintance, a musician, an artist, a fellow-*intsumiso*, pierced or punked-out but *euskaldun*, Basque-speaking, more often than not. And you could end up going on down the street together, even doing a *gau-pasa*—an all-nighter (a demi-satirical song he wrote three years ago began, "My name is Kirmen Uribe, / a.k.a. Let's Celebrate. . . . I often go out by moonlight / and go to bed by day," a song that was a snap to translate since I'd participated in a Kutxi *gau-pasa* once or twice). Otherwise, even a block and a half from Kutxi, there was tranquillity, and you could, as Uribe did, read and think in peace, and get work done.

While he was doing his dissertation on the Basque poet Xabier

Lizardi, Uribe was writing lyrics for a number of folk and rock musicians. The novelist Anjel Lertxundi later published a wry young-adult book, illustrated by the brilliant Basque cartoon-artist Antton Olariaga, in which Uribe appears, the narrator being a teenage groupie-*paparazza*, smitten. At the end of the book, Kirmen Uribe himself goes to visit her class at school, and discusses a song lyric, to great effect. He said in an interview recently that he probably wouldn't have dared to write poetry at all if he hadn't written song lyrics first. When the Spanish translation of *Bitartean heldu eskutik (Meanwhile Take My Hand)* came out, in the spring of 2004, he said—for the first time in public, as he remarked—that what actually first made him start writing was his older brother's giving him a copy of Leonard Cohen's "A Spicebox of Earth" when he was thirteen.

In 2000, Uribe began working with several musicians on an oral-history project, loosely defined—collecting stories and local folk songs from coast towns like Ondarroa, turning the stories into poems or lyrics, which the musicians, Mikel Urdangarin and Bingen Mendizabal, set to music. The poems "Visit," "The Island," and "Loren" all first appeared in the 2001 CD-chapbook, *Bar Puerto,* that documented the project. No one who can write a clear sentence in Euskara remains unemployed for long in the Basque Country. Uribe was scriptwriting for ETB-1, the Basque-language public-television station at the time, as he would until 2003; in 1999 the Basque-language daily, *Egunkaria,* had employed him to write a weekly 300-word column, for which he came up with a distilled yet conversational two-paragraph form that could seemingly contain anything, from a snatch of dialogue in a coffee shop, through a story about Robert Louis Stevenson's widow, or Czeslaw Milosz, or a boxing match, to a quirk of Ondarroan usage or a retold folk tale.

When *Bitartean heldu eskutik* was first published, in the fall of 2001, it went into a second printing within a month. Uribe found out in the middle of the following year that a Madrid publishing house would bring out a Spanish translation, which he did in collaboration with the poet Gerardo Markuleta and the critic Ana Arregi. When

Mientras tanto dame la mano came out two years later in a bilingual edition, it, too, went into a second printing after a month.

/

After these English translations had begun appearing in magazines in the U.S., in the late fall of 2002, Kirmen told me he was thinking of coming to New York the following March. As things turned out, the two *Bar Puerto* musicians decided to come along, with a rock-guitarist friend, Rafa Rueda; and a half-dozen planned bilingual readings became bilingual reading-concerts. The Iraq war began in the middle of their trip, and Kirmen asked for a rush translation of "Bad Dream." The month before, the Spanish government had shut down the Basque-language newspaper *Egunkaria* (in a case that has yet to be clarified and may yet end up shelved); we read "No Saying" several times, as presciently appropriate. At CUNY Hostos Community College, in the South Bronx, a student from Central America shyly asked them how to say "Thank you," then stumbled through it: "*E-s-k-e-r-r-i-k . . . a-s-k-o, a todos ustedes.*" Thank you all.

"Longing, but not beyond knowing what contentment is," a New York friend said to me after one of the evenings in Manhattan: the feeling he'd picked up from the whole, he meant. I heard it as a descant on a line from "The Island": "Sunday on the beach for all people of good desires." When they'd gone back home, I happened to hear Uribe and Urdangarin being interviewed about the trip, over Basque public radio online, and at one point Uribe said, "In that city of 10,000 languages, not a single person asked us why, if we knew Spanish, we were doing our work in Basque."

Within six months of the trip, they had put together a trilingual (Basque/Spanish/English) CD-size illustrated book with music, called *Zaharregia txikiegia agian / Una manera de mirar / Too Old, Too Small, Maybe.* In it, poems alternated with watercolor takes (by the artist Mikel Valverde, who in March had come along for the ride, bringing his sketchbook) of New York cityscapes, Basque Country landscapes, and a few conceptual whimsies. Although none of the poems remarked on the trip directly, all but three of fourteen pieces were new since March. (Of the fourteen, "The Cuckoo," "I Love You, No," "Things That Are Perfect," "Notes on a Loose Piece of Paper," and "Don't Make It a Choice" appear here; "The Gold Ring," which Uribe had brought to New York in prose, had become a poem.)

/

In a foreword to *Zaharregia,* Uribe wrote of having been struck by a remark the American poet Phillis Levin made to him after one evening:

> She said that she'd heard of Euskara before as well, she'd seen things written in Basque. She'd looked them over and more than once had tried to read them, just to see if she could. She was wonderstruck at all the *x*'s that turned up on the page. *The language looks like a treasure map,* she said to me. *If you just forget all the rest of the letters and focus in on the* x, *it looks as if you could find out where the treasure is.* I thought it was the most beautiful thing one could say about a language one didn't know, that it's the map to a treasure.

Uribe had spent a year in Trento, Italy, doing comparative-literature postgraduate studies at the university there, in the late 1990s, and had traveled elsewhere in Europe. During the New York trip he wrote in a travel diary:

> Distance is necessary in order to make any forward progress, to become aware of your mistakes, to be able to take a backward look. A poet has to be able to view the world as a whole, and also able to master its smallest detail inside out, simultaneously close up but separate. He needs that distance, and also a love for the human person holed up in their privatest corner.

/

I've placed the emphasis I have on the landscapes here since, in the poems, they are mostly conveyed in two- or three-word gestures.

After all, everyone reading in Basque can be presumed to know exactly how Basque landscapes look. Likewise, even now, while having my own understanding of the first poem I translated from *Bitartean*—"Memory Exercise," since I was fascinated to see Raymond Carver turn up in a poem in Basque—I cannot be sure if any native *euskaldun* would ever hear it in the precise way I do. From these poems of Kirmen Uribe's I learn what it's like to have lived your whole life unmistakably surrounded by a situation—the *gatazka*, as it's called in Basque, "the dispute." The poems convey—far more clearly than any of the political actors in the Basque Country or Spain ever seem to do (and particularly those who've used what has been called speechless speech, or violence in place of words)—what the situation actually is. As demands go, there's a lot to be said for the simple sensation of freedom inherent in "I'm going to stay here," in the poem "Don't Make It a Choice."

A Note on This Translation

The section breaks here follow those of the original Basque edition, published by Susa Argitaletxea (Zarautz, Spain) in 2001. In the Spanish edition, published by Visor (Madrid) in 2004, an extra epigraph appeared, below the John Keats on the second half-title page, from the Brazilian writer Clarice Lispector, above the subscript "Epitaph etched on her tomb": "To take someone's hand was / what I always hoped for from happiness." Between the two editions, some poems were removed and other poems added. The order of poems here remains the same as that of the 2004 Spanish edition for the most part. "Loren," for example, was left out of the Spanish edition; I've restored it here, though in a different place (in the original, it fell in the second section, like "Danger," which it followed there as well). "The Beech Tree" preceded "Way Off There." The quotations on the epigraph pages, except for those from Keats and other writers in English, are my translations of Uribe's versions in Euskara.

"False Acacia" and "Birds in Winter" were both finished after the Spanish edition had gone to the printer, early in 2004. "Anus mundi," which Uribe has allowed me to use as an afterword, first appeared as a column in the Basque newspaper *Berria* (*Egunkaria's* replacement) on Saturday, March 13, 2004, two days after the al-Qaeda rail-station bombings in Madrid, and so was written at a moment when the central government, despite mounting evidence to the contrary, was still insistently airing its conviction that Basques, the Basque separatist group ETA, had been behind the attacks. (A stance that helped contribute, in my opinion, to its being voted out of power on that Sunday, once the evidence had at last been acknowledged.) For me, the three pieces triangulated and, together, suggested reasons to be deeply hopeful.

As for questions of language, my readings here have perhaps had as much to do with my changing relationship to Euskara, which I didn't encounter firsthand until 1999, as with my relationship to the work itself. Most of all and throughout, I wanted to make sure these were poems in some kindred form of our own English. Or in some kindred tone, at least. "The Aresti-Duchamp Chess Game," for instance, is written in *hika*, the vertiginous Basque intimate "you," which though it exists in Unified Basque, is not often used by *euskaldunberriak*—new Basque-speakers. In *hika*, the second-person verb in a sentence changes according to the sex of the person you're speaking to, and *hika* also causes the rest of the verbs in the sentence to change in tandem, as if always to refer to that "you." I like to imagine Kirmen imagining the French artist Duchamp in *hika* with the *euskaldunberri* poet Aresti over their chessboard, and dreaming up the Groucho-and-Harpo pas-de-deux handshake between them at the end. For an equivalent of *hika* in English, I tried to rely on the diction of my uncles and male cousins in Dakota, Rice, and Otter Tail Counties, Minnesota. Not an entirely arbitrary choice.

Regarding license: In the poem "The Fishbowl," the phrase *bira eta bira* simply means "circling round and around," but had attractions so strong to the ear, and felt so visible to the eye (even though *"eta"* as a word is "and"), that it demanded to be present, though there are, of course, many other fish still circling round and around in other fishbowls in unilateral and oblivious ways. As I write this, ETA has declared a permanent ceasefire, so there's hope.

The requirements of a language whose syntax is in many ways upside down from that of English impelled me to use any means available to make a tightly moving thought-train clear; in some cases this involved breaking lines differently and changing the shape of a poem so that it would fall as naturally on an American English page as it does on the Basque one.

The whole process of working on these poems has often felt like jamming, and "The Language of the Animals" is a lineated riff I did on a column Kirmen wrote for *Berria* in the summer of 2005; we decided it was fine for the original to remain in prose as written.

Elizabeth Macklin
March 2006

Meanwhile / Take My Hand

This living hand, now warm and capable
Of earnest grasping, would, if it were cold
And in the icy silence of the tomb,
So haunt thy days and chill thy dreaming nights
That thou wouldst wish thine own heart dry of blood
So in my veins red life might stream again,
And thou be conscience-calmed—see here it is—
       I hold it towards you.

                JOHN KEATS

Ibaia

Garai batean ibaia zen hemen
baldosak eta bankuak dauden tokian.
Dozena bat ibai baino gehiago daude hiriaren azpian,
zaharrenei kasu eginez gero.
Orain langile auzo bateko plaza besterik ez da.
Eta hiru makal dira ibaiak hor
azpian jarraitzen duen seinale bakar.

Denok dugu barruan uhola dakarren ibai estali bat.
Ez badira beldurrak, damuak dira.
Ez badira zalantzak, ezinak.

Mendebaleko haizeak astintzen ditu makalak.
Nekez egiten du oinez jendeak.
Laugarren pisuan emakume nagusi bat
leihotik arropak botatzen ari da:
alkandora beltza bota du eta gona kuadroduna
eta zetazko zapi horia eta galtzerdiak
eta herritik iritsi zen neguko egun hartan
soinean zeramatzan txarolezko zapata zuribeltzak.
Hegabera izoztuak ematen zuten bere oinek elurretan.

Haurrak arropen atzetik joan dira arineketan.
Ezkontzako soinekoa atera du azkenik,
makal batean pausatu da baldar,
txori pisuegi bat balitz bezala.

Zarata handi bat entzun da. Izutu egin dira oinezkoak.
Haizeak errotik atera du makaletako bat.
Zuhaitzaren erroek emakume nagusi baten eskua dirudite,
beste esku batek noiz laztanduko zain.

The River

There was a time a river ran through here,
there where the benches and the paving start.
A dozen rivers more underlie the city
if you believe the oldest citizens.
Now it's a square in the workers' quarter,
that's all, three poplars the only sign
the river underneath keeps running.

In everyone here is a hidden river that brings floods.
If they are not fears, they're contritions.
If they are not doubts, inabilities.

The west wind has been shaking the poplars,
people barely make their way along on foot.
From her fourth-floor window an older woman
is throwing articles of clothing.
She's hurled a black shirt, a plaid skirt,
the yellow silk scarf and the stockings
and the black-and-white patent-leather shoes
she wore the winter day she came in from her town.
In the snow they looked like frozen lapwings.

Children have gone racing after the clothing.
The wedding dress exited last,
has been clumsy and perched on a branch,
too heavy a bird.

We've heard a loud noise. The passersby have been startled.
The wind has lifted a poplar out by its roots.
They could be an older woman's hand
awaiting any other hand's caressing.

/ 5 /

One / Bat

Your body is not a word,
it does not lie or
speak truth either.

MARGARET ATWOOD

Irla

Horixe da zoriona,
orduka lan egiten duen behargina.

ANNE SEXTON

Igandea da hondartzan asmo oneko jendearentzat.
Hango harrabots urruna entzuten da irlatik.

Uretara sartu gara biluzik,
Anemonak, trikuak, barbarinak ikusi ditugu hondoan.
Begira, haizeak garia bezala mugitzen du urak hondarra.
Urpera sartu eta azpitik begiratu zaitut.
Atsegin dut esku eta zangoen mugimendu geldoa,
Atsegin sabelpeek itsasbelarren forma hartzean.

Lehorrera igo gara. Bero da eta itzal egiten dute pinuek.
Gaziak dira zure besoak, gazia bularra, sabela gazia.
Ilargia itsasoarekin lotzen duen indar berak lotu gaitu geu ere.
Mendeak segundu bihurtu dira eta segunduak mende.
Udare zurituak gure gorputzak.

Anemonak, trikuak, barbarinak ikusi ditugu hondoan.
Igandea da hondartzan asmo oneko jendearentzat.

The Island

So this is happiness,
that journeyman.

ANNE SEXTON

It's Sunday on the beach for all people of good desires.
You can hear the faraway noise of it from the island.

We go into the water naked,
We see anemones, red mullets, sea thistle on the bay floor.
Look—like the wind the wheat the water moves the sand.
I go under and behold you from underneath.
I like the slow movement of your hands and legs.
I like your underbelly's taking the form of seaweed.

We go up on dry land. It's hot and the pines make shadow.
Your arms are salty, your chest salty, belly salty.
The same power that joins the moon with the sea
      has joined us, too.
Centuries become a second and seconds centuries.
Our bodies, peeled pears.

We see anemones, red mullets, sea thistle on the bay floor.
It's Sunday on the beach for all people of good desires.

Bisita

Heroina larrua jotzea bezain gozoa zela
esaten zuen garai batean.

Medikuek esaten dute okerrera ez duela egin,
eguna joan eguna etorri, eta lasai hartzeko.
Hilabetea da berriro esnatu ez dela
azken ebakuntzaz geroztik.

Hala ere egunero egiten diogu bisita
Arreta Intentsiboko Unitateko seigarren kutxara.
Aurreko oheko gaisoa negar batean aurkitu dugu gaur,
inor ez zaiola bisitara agertu diotso erizainari.

Hilabetea arrebaren hitzik entzun ez dugula.
Ez dut lehen bezala bizitza osoa aurretik ikusten,
esaten zigun,
ez dut promesarik nahi, ez dut damurik nahi,
maitasun keinu bat besterik ez.

Amak eta biok soilik hitz egiten diogu.
Anaiak lehen ez zion gauza handirik esaten,
orain ez da agertu ere egiten.
Aita atean geratzen da, isilik.

Ez dut gauez lorik egiten, esaten zigun arrebak,
beldur diot loak hartzeari, beldur amesgaiztoei.
Orratzek min egiten didate eta hotz naiz,
hotza zabaltzen dit sueroak zainetan zehar.

Visit

Heroin had been as sweet as sex
she used to say, at one time.

The doctors have been saying now she won't get worse,
to go day by day, take things easy.
It's been a month since she failed to wake up
after the last operation.

Still and all, we go every day to visit her
in Cubicle Six of the Intensive Care Unit.
Today we found the patient in the bed beside hers
in tears, no one had come to visit, he'd said to the nurse.

An entire month and we haven't heard a word from my sister.
I don't see my whole life stretching before me the way I did,
she used to tell us.
I don't want promises, I don't want repentance,
just some sign of love is all.

Our mother and I are the ones who talk to her.
Our brother, with her, never said too much,
and here doesn't make an appearance.
Our father hangs back in the doorway, silent.

I don't sleep nights, she used to tell us,
I'm afraid to go to sleep, afraid of the bad dreams.
The needles hurt me and I'm cold,
the serum sends the cold through every one of my veins.

Gorputz ustel honi ihes egingo banio.

Bitartean heldu eskutik, eskatzen zigun,
ez dut promesarik nahi, ez dut damurik nahi,
maitasun keinu bat besterik ez.

If I could only escape from this rotten body.

Meanwhile take my hand, she implored us,
I don't want promises, I don't want repentance,
just some sign of love is all.

Arriskua

Arriskua zenuen maite.
Zenbaiten ustean haurtzaro latzak
betiko markatu zizkizun esku ahurretako erreka lehorrak,
eta horregatik mugak hauste hori,
bazterrera, zulora hurbiltzeko joera.

Irlandatik, Danimarkatik zetozen kamioiak arraina biltzera.
Atzeko kolpe-leungailura abantean igo eta
abiada hartzen zutenean jauzi egitea zenuen gogoko,
hirulau urrats egin eta lurrera erortzeko.

Bonba zaharrak hartzen zenituen eskuan,
gerra zaharreko frontean erdietsiak,
sasi artean lubakiak antzematen ziren,
ezin sendatuzko zauri sakonegiak bezala.

Arriskua zenuen maite,
eta konturatu naiz ezer ez garela arriskurik gabe,
atea zeharkatzerik ez, itsasoratzerik ez, maitalerik ez.
Denbora igaro da urte haietatik
eta, gaur, zure akabera aurreratzen zutenen begiak
neguak hildako kardantxiloenak dira.

Danger

You loved danger.
Some people think a tough childhood
marked your palms' dry creekbeds forever,
and thus your breaking through borders,
that propensity to gravitate to fringes, holes.

The trucks came from Ireland, from Denmark, to load fish.
You liked to climb on their tailgates
and—as they picked up speed—to jump,
in three, four steps, and hit the dirt.

You picked up old bombs bare-handed,
come by on the old war front,
in the underbrush we found the trenches,
like wounds too deep, unable to heal.

You loved danger,
and I realize we're nothing at all without danger:
can't go through a door, go to sea, no lovers.
Time has passed since those years,
and today, the eyes of those who predicted your death
are the eyes of winter-killed finches.

Loren

Lehorreratu dira ontziak,
korrikan doaz umeak.
Lorenek gorriz du ilea,
oinetan takoiak.

Cocacolakin whiskya eta
elur malutar patrikan.
Hari segiko dionik ez da
jaio mundu zabalean.

Nola egin duzu, esan diote,
soineko hori josteko?
Oihal beltzean klarion zuriz
izarrak marraztu ditut.

Min egiten du ipar haizeak
ene aurpegian.
Min egiten du
sortu ez den mundu berriak.

Loren

The boats have come in,
the kids race down.
Loren has got red hair now,
wears spike heels.

Whiskey and Coke,
in her pocket, snow.
No one's been born on Earth
to keep up with her.

How, they ask her,
did you make that dress?
On black cloth with white chalk
I drew the stars.

The wind from the North
hurts my face.
The new world as yet unmade
hurts, too.

Pagoa

Altzoko Imazek pagoa landatu zuen
Basaitz mendian, andrea ezagututako urtean.

Bizitza osoan arretaz egin zion kontu,
gerrikoarekin neurria hartuz lantzean-lantzean.

Pello Errotaren esanetan bertso jartzen puntakoetarik,
andrea baino 25 egun lehenago zendu zen, 1893an.

Pagoari zabalera hartzeko, gaur egun
bost metroko gerrikoa beharko luke agian.

The Beech Tree

Imaz of Altzo planted a beech tree
on Basaitz Mountain, the year he met his wife.

His whole life, he kept track of the tree with care,
measuring it against his belt, from time to time.

Pello Errota said he was among the best of poets.
He passed on, in 1893, 25 days before his wife.

To measure the breadth of the beech, nowadays
he might have needed a belt some five yards long.

Mohammed

Aipa nezake lehenik ama, Assia arreba gaztea,
eta Aita, besamotza eta edadetua, etxeko patioan.
Aipa nitzake zerurik zabalenak, albaraka lurrina,
laranja urez bustitako eskuak.

Aipa nezake Kotimo, lagunik minena, handia eta umoretsua.
Nola ikusten genuen telebista elkarrekin,
nola egiten genuen eskolak ihesi Tangerreko molletara joateko,
nola imajinatzen genituen Londres, Amsterdam edo New York,
portuko urazalaren gasolina orbanetan.

Bada behin eta berriz entzun dudan kontakizun bat.
Aitak kontatzen zigun txikitan.
Toledo izeneko hiri bat aipatzen zuen,
bazela hiri hartan dorre bat,
eta dorrean ate bat hogeita lau giltzarrapoz kondenatua.
Kontatzen zigun errege bat hil bakoitzean
beste giltzarrapo bat jartzen zuela errege berriak,
aurrekoen ohiturari jarraituz.
Hogeita bosgarren erregeari jakinminak gehiago egin zion,
eta erreinuko jakintsuen esanei muzin eginez
giltzarrapoak banan banan kendu eta atea zabaltzeko agindu zuen.
Mundu guztiaren harridurarako,
dorre barruan margo batzuk besterik ez zituzten aurkitu.
Horixe zen hango altxor guztia.
Margoek soldadu arabeak irudikatzen zituzten, zaldiak, gameluak.
Eta azken margoan gaztigu hau:
ate hau zabaltzean soldadu arabeek hartuko dute hiria.

Mohammed

I could mention my mother first, my little sister Assia,
and Father, older, missing an arm, in the yard at home.
I could mention the widest of skies, the perfume of basil,
the hands wet with orange juice.

I could mention Kotimo, my closest friend, large and amused.
How we watched TV together, how we skipped school
to go to the Tangiers docklands,
how we imagined London, Amsterdam, New York
in the gasoline stains on the surface of the harbor water.

There's a story I've heard time and again.
Father told it to us when we were little.
It made mention of a city called Toledo,
how in that city there was a tower,
and in the tower a door sealed under twenty-four padlocks.
He told us that each time a king died
the new king would add a new padlock,
following the custom of his forebears.
Curiosity got the better of the twenty-fifth king,
and scorning the counsels of the realm's wise men
he ordered the padlocks removed one by one and the door opened.
To the amazement of all,
in the tower they found nothing but a few paintings.
That was the whole of the treasure there.
The paintings pictured Arab soldiers, horses, camels.
And in the last painting this reckoning:
When this door opens, Arab soldiers will take the city.

Ilundu orduko sartu zen Tariq b. Ziyad Toledoko hirian,
eta berehala hil zuen bertako erregea,
jakinminak gehiago egin zion errege hura.

Aitaren kontakizuna nuen gogoan Tangerretik Cadizerako bidean.
Europako gerra batean galdu zuen besoa aitak.
Esaten zuen ez zegoela ezer itsasoaz bestalde,
kentzeko asmo horiek burutik, zahar sentitzen zela,
laguntza behar zutela etxea gobernatzeko.

Aipa nezake gauez atera ginela Tangerretik,
hogeita lau ordu luze behar izan genituela Cadizera heltzeko.
Aipa nezake ehun eta berrogeita hamar mila
kobratu zigula patroiak bidaiaren truke.
Eta berrogei gehiago, poliziak ikusi gabe
hondartzatik aterako gintuela agindu zigun alproja hark,
dirua hartu baina gure bila agertu ez zen berak.

Gero etorri ziren Madril, Bartzelona, Bordele, Bilbo.
Eraikinak, denda handiak, galsoro lehorrak.
Baita gaua eta alkohola ere
eta pikuak bezala urtzen ziren gorputz lirainak.

Bada behin eta berriz burura datorkidan amesgaizto bat,
amesgaiztorik latzena. Benetan jazoriko horiek baitira latzenak.
Ezin ahantz dezaket Kotimo, liskar batean hila
hondartzako alproja harekin topo egin ondoren.
Zorigaitzaren kontuak.
Ezin ahantz, berrogei mila horiengatik
egin zutela bat komun hartan odolak eta elurrak.

Near nightfall Tariq bin Ziyad entered the city of Toledo,
and had soon slain the king of that place,
that king whose curiosity had got the better of him.

I thought of Father's story as we crossed from Tangiers to Cádiz.
Father lost his arm in a European war.
He used to say there was nothing on the other side of the sea,
to get those thoughts out of my head, he felt old,
they needed help running the household.

I could mention that we left Tangiers at night,
it took us twenty-four long hours to reach Cádiz.
I could mention the hundred and fifty thousand
pesetas the captain charged us for the passage.
And the extra forty, for that swine who promised
to get us off the beach past the police,
and took the money but didn't show up for us.

Then came Madrid, Barcelona, Bordeaux, Bilbao.
Buildings, the big stores, dry wheat fields.
And the night, and alcohol,
and sleek bodies melting like ripe figs.

There's a nightmare that comes to mind time and again,
one fierce nightmare. Of the fiercest kind.
I can't forget Kotimo, dead in a fight
when we ran into that swine from the beach.
Facts of bad luck.
I can't forget how for the sake of that forty thousand
blood and snow intermixed in that bathroom.

Patioan utzi ditut lagunak. Galerietarantz egin dut.
Urrun da albaraka lurrina, urrun laranja-urez bustiriko eskuak.
Burdinazko ateak zeharkatzen ari da labanderiako gurditxoa.
Begira egoten naiz horrelakoetan.
Barrote artetik kaleko atea ere ikusten dut suerterik bada.
Ongi zenbatuak ditut hemendik kalera dauden ateak.

Hogeita lau giltzarrapo besterik ez dira.

I've left my friends in the yard, and head off to the cellblocks.
The perfume of basil is far away, the hands wet with orange juice.
The little laundry cart is passing through the iron doors.
I wait and see, at such times.
Between bars I glimpse the street door, too, with any luck.
I've counted and recounted the doors from here to the street.

They're twenty-four padlocks and nothing more.

Maite Zaitut, Ez

Berrogei urtez labe garaietan lan egin arren,
barru-barrutik,
baserritarra izaten jarraitzen zuen.

Urrian, etxeko balkoian
soldagailuarekin
piper gorriak erretzen zituen.

Denak isilarazten zituen
haren ahots ozenak.
Alabak egiten zion soilik aurre.

Ez zuen inoiz maite zaitut esaten.

Tabakoak eta altzairuaren hautsak
ahots-kordak urratu zizkioten.
Mitxoleta bi hostoak galtzen.

Alaba beste hiri batera ezkondu zen.
Erretiratuak oparia zekarren.
Ez errubirik, zeta gorririk ezta ere.

Urtetan lantegitik ebatsi zituen piezak.
Soldagailuarekin
altzairuzko ohea josi zuen, ezari-ezarian.

Ez zuen inoiz maite zaitut esaten.

I Love You, No

Even though he worked in the steel mills
in those times, through and through
he remained a farmer.

In October, he'd roast the red peppers
on the balcony at home
with the acetylene torch.

His sounding voice
silenced everyone.
His daughter stood up to him.

He never said I love you.

Tobacco and steel dust
plowed through his vocal cords.
A field poppy less two leaves.

His daughter has married into another city.
The retiree brings a gift.
Not rubies, not red silk, either.

Over the years he lifted the parts from the mill.
With the acetylene torch
inch by inch he made her a bed from the steel.

He never said I love you.

Kardiograma

—Deskriba iezadazu bere bihotza.
—Laku izoztu bat ematen du,
        eta behin izan zen haurraren aurpegia
        ezabatzen ari da bertan.

Cardiogram

—Describe, if you would, his heart for me.
—It's like a frozen lake,
       and the face of the child that he once was
       is erasing itself in there.

Two / Bi

The loveliest stories are childhood ones.
This is my favorite: Once, I swallowed a
bone button. That day my mother cried.

ZBIGNIEW HERBERT

Gerraostea

Antzarak igaro dira urrian magal bipiletatik.
Haurrak konturatu eta korrika doaz atzetik.
"Ezkontza, ezkontza" egiten dute oihu.
"Puntako biak ezkongaiak dira"
esan dio neskatiletako batek ahizpa gazteari,
"eta hegaletakoak gonbidatuak".

Antzarak igaro dira urrian magal bipiletatik.
Korrika doaz haurrak atzetik.
Adokin bustietan beren oin biluziek
negu gorria aurreratzen dute.
"Ezkontza, ezkontza".

Postwar

In October geese passed the pillaged laps.
It dawns on the children and they run after.
"Wedlock, wedlock," they yell running.
"The two at the head are the newlyweds,"
a small girl says to her younger sister,
"and the rest of the flock are guests at the wedding."

In October geese passed the pillaged laps.
The children go running after.
On the wet cobbles their bare feet
anticipate the hard winter.

"Wedlock, wedlock."

Txoriak neguan

Txoriak salbatzea zen gure misioa.
Elurretan preso geratu ziren txoriak salbatzea.

Hondartza aldean egoten ziren gordeta gehienak
    itsaso beltzaren abarora.
Txoriak ere beltzak ziren.
Babeslekutik atera eta etxera eramaten genituen
    patrikaretan sartuta.
Txori txiki-txikiak, gure haur eskuetan ere
    doi-doi sartzen zirela.

Gero, berogailuaren ondoan jartzen genituen.
Txoriek baina ez zuten luzaroan irauten.
Bi edo hiru orduren buruan hil egiten ziren.
Guk ez genuen ulertzen zergatik,
ez genuen ulertzen haien esker txarra.
Izan ere, esnetan bustitako ogi apurrak ematen genizkien
    jatera ahora
eta ohea ere prestatzen genien
gure bufandarik koloretsuenekin.

Alferrik baina, hil egiten ziren.

Gurasoek haserre, esaten ziguten
ez ekartzeko txori gehiago etxera,
hil egiten zirela gehiegizko beroagatik.
Eta natura jakintsua dela
iritsiko zela udaberria bere txoriekin.

Gu pentsakor jartzen ginen une batez,
beharbada gurasoak zuzen izango dira.

Birds in Winter

Saving the birds was our mission that whole winter.
Saving the birds imprisoned in the snow.

All along the beach most of them were hidden,
    nestled in the shade of the black sea.
The birds were black, too.
From the coverts we'd take them and carry them home
    in our coat pockets.
The tiniest birds, barely contained
    in even our child-sized hands.

Later, we'd lay them beside the warm stove.
But the birds never lasted long.
In two or three hours they died.
We didn't see why,
didn't understand their bad luck.
After all, we'd given them
breadcrumbs moistened in milk,
    held to their mouths, to eat,
and furnished a nest for each
with our most colorful winter scarves.
But it was useless, they kept on dying.

Furious, our parents told us
not to bring home any more birds,
they were dying of too much heat.
And that nature is wise,
spring would come with its own birds.

We sat and considered their statements,
it could be that they will be right.

Hala eta guztiz ere,
biharamonean berriro joango ginen hondartza aldera
    txoriak salbatzera.
Gure ahalegina
itsasoan elurra bezain alferrekoa zela jakin arren.

Eta txoriek hiltzen jarraitzen zuten, txoriek hiltzen.

Still and all, the very next day
we would flock off back to the beach
        to save the birds,
though we knew
it was fruitless as snow in the sea.

And our birds kept dying, these birds taking life.

Gereziondoa

Hil egin da etxeko gereziondoa,
lorean zegoela leihotik begiratzen genuen hura,
gogan al duzu?
Hain xinglea itsaso handiaren ondoan.

Gereziondoa zuhaitz minbera da.
Hala esan zuen osabak, badakizu,
ernanien habiak non zeuden esaten zigun hark.
Gereziondoak ez du gehienetan
hogeita bost baino askoz urte gehiago betetzen.

Etxeko zakurra ere hil egin da.
Tira, albaitariak hil zuen txerto batekin.
Zoratu egin zen goizetik gauera zakurra.
Hasieran, ez zuen etxolatik irten nahi.
Gero ardiak akatzen hasi zen eta etxekoei hozka egiten.

Zu hil eta egun gutxira hil ziren.

The Cherry Tree

The cherry tree at home has died,
the one we'd stare at from the window
when it was in bloom, can you see it?
Infinitely fragile beside the huge sea.

The cherry is a temperamental tree.
So said our uncle, you know,
the one who used to tell us
where the swallows' nests were.
A cherry tree most times does not
make it much beyond twenty-five years.

The dog at home has gone and died, too.
Or, the vet killed him with an injection.
He went crazy the whole day long, the dog.
At first he didn't want to leave his doghouse.
Then began lighting into the sheep and biting the family.

Not many days after you died, they died.

Teknologia

Aitonak ez zekien irakurtzen,
ez zekien idazten. Hala ere kontalari

ezaguna zen herrian. Berak pizten zituen,
haurrez inguraturik, sanjuan suak.

Aitaren kaligrafia etzana zen, jantzia.
Doiki ehuntzen zuen papera,

arbela zizelatuko balu bezala.
Mahaian dut soldaduzkatik igorritako postala.

"Yo bien, tú bien
mándame cien".

Gure sasoian mezu elektronikoak
bidaltzen dizkiogu elkarri.

Hiru belaunalditan, egia da,
idazketaren historia luzea igaro dugu.

Dena den, kezkak, beldurrak
beti-betikoak dira, eta izango.

"Yo bien, tú bien. . ."

Technology

My grandfather didn't know how to read,
he didn't know how to write. He was, however,

a storyteller famous in the village. It was he who lit,
surrounded by children, the Midsummer bonfires.

My father's handwriting was cursive, spruce.
He meticulously interlaced the paper,

as if he were engraving slate.
On my desk is a postcard he sent from the service:

"Yo bien, tú bien,
mándame cien."
("I well, you well,
send a few bills.")

In these times of ours, e-mails
are what we send each other.

In three generations, true,
we've traveled the long history of writing.

Nonetheless, worries, fears
are the same as ever, and will be:

"Yo bien, tú bien. . ."

John Keats-en hilartitzaz

Idatzi neure izena ere urarekin
euriak zehazten ditu-eta
gurean gizakion ziluetak.

After John Keats's Gravestone

Write my name in water, too,
since in our land it's rain
that defines our human outlines.

Three / *Hiru*

Our games are done, love, let's go to bed.
On tiptoe. Our billowing nightshirts white.
Papa and Mama will say they're hearing
    spirits
when we trade our breaths at night.

INGEBORG BACHMANN

Arima gaiztoak

Amaren amona hartu dut gogoan.
Bazuen arima errarien berri.
Bazekien, goizean suaren hausterrei erreparatuz gero
gauez arima gaiztoak ala parte onekoak ibili ziren.

Behin, baltseotik bueltan,
etxetik kanpo aurkitu zuten amak eta ahizpek.
Etxera ez sartzeko agindu zien,
kamisoia soinean eta argizaria eskuan,
han barruan arima gaiztoren bat zebilelako.

Oheko maindireei erreparatu diet goizean.
Zure usaina darie eta zure zainetako ur arrastoak dituzte.
Zure arimaren aztarnak.

Gaiztoa ala parte onekoa zen ez dakit.
Horregatik, errito zaharrak artoski errepikatuz,
bart entzun genuen musika jarri dut berriro,
eta ohera sartu ezari-ezarian.
Maindireak estutu ditut nire kontra,
azala laztandu,
eta gogora ekarri ostera ere, bata bestearen atzetik,
bart gaueko mugimendu oro.

Izan dut zure arimaren berri.
Zalantzarik gabe, gaizto horietakoa da.

Evil Spirits

I'm remembering my mother's grandmother.
She had knowledge of wandering souls.
Mornings she knew, having considered the ashes in the grate,
whether evil or good souls had walked by night.

Once, coming home from a dance,
Mother and her sisters found her outdoors.
"Don't go in," she commanded,
in only her nightdress, candle in hand:
one of the evil kind was loose in there.

This morning I consider the sheets on my bed.
Your smell rises from them, they show signs of you.
Traces of your soul.

Whether it was evil or good I don't know.
And so, repeating the olden rites with care,
I put on the music we heard last night
and slip by slow degrees into bed.
I hug the sheets to myself,
stroke their finish,
and bring fresh to mind, one by one,
every single movement of this past night.

I've had knowledge of your soul.
It's one of the evil kind, doubtless.

Sagarrak

Homerok hitz bakarra zerabilen gorputza eta azala izendatzeko.
Safok lagunen bularretan hartzen zuen lo.
Etxeparek emazte biluzgorriekin egiten zuen amets.

Aspaldi isildu ziren denak.

Gaur badirudi perfektuak izan behar dugula ohean ere,
supermerkatuko sagar gorri horiek bezala, perfektuegiak.
Larregi eskatzen diogu geure buruari
eta norberaz, ondokoaz
espero duguna ez da ia sekula gertatzen.
Legeak bestelakoak dira gorputzak korapilatzean.

Homerok hitz bakarra zerabilen gorputza eta azala izendatzeko.
Safok lagunen bularretan hartzen zuen lo.
Etxeparek emazte biluzgorriekin egiten zuen amets.

Gogoan dut oraindik
elkarri besarkatuta lo egiten genuen garaia,
tigrekume ikaratiak gu, gaubeilan.

Apples

Homer used a single word for body and skin.
Sappho slept on the breasts of her friends.
Etxepare dreamt of stark-naked women.

All of them silent for ages now.

Today it seems we have to be perfect in bed, too,
like those red apples in the supermarket,
too perfect.
We're asking too much of ourselves,
and what we hope for
from any of us, nearest neighbors,
almost never happens.
The laws are different when bodies tangle.

Homer used a single word for body and skin.
Sappho slept on the breasts of her friends.
Etxepare dreamt of stark-naked women.

Still I have in my mind
that epoch when we slept holding each other,
scared tiger cubs in our vigil.

Musua

Nire titiak txikiak dira eta begiak biribilak.
Zure zangoak, luzeak eta freskuak
iturritik behera datorren zurrusta bezala.
Hozka egin dizut zaman,
sendoa duzu, heldu gabea oraindik,
intxaur erori berriaren antzeko.
Nire gainera igo zara eta musuka hasi sabelean,
uhin umelak barreiatu dizkidazu azalean,
orain hemen, gero han,
ekaitza hasi baino lehen erortzen diren
lehen tanta lodiek bezala, pla, pla, pla.

Lo geratu gara bizkar eta bular,
biltzen diren moduan ezpainak
hasperenaren ostean.

The Kiss

My breasts are small and my eyes round.
Your legs long and cool as the freshet
that runs down from the fountain.
I bite your neck,
it's sturdy, still not yet ripe,
like a walnut that has just now fallen.
You clamber on top, start kissing my middle,
strew wet wavelets all over my skin,
now up here, now down there,
like the first fat drops to fall before
the storm starts, splat, splat, splat.

We've gone to sleep back to chest,
the way lips rejoin
after sighing.

Zuhaitzen denbora

Zugan da zuhaitzen denbora
elkar maitatu ondoren.

Ohean lo, betazalek
soilik estaltzen zaituzte.

Ez jarraitu beldurrari,
ez esan beti, ez esan inoiz ez,
utzi libre munduari
bidea egiten.

Zugan da zuhaitzen denbora
elkar maitatu ondoren.

Plazer-urak biltzen zaitu
malkoak begia legez.

Ez jarraitu beldurrari,
ez esan beti, ez esan inoiz ez,
utzi libre munduari
bidea egiten.

Zugan da zuhaitzen denbora
elkar maitatu ondoren.

The Space-Time of Trees

The space-time of trees is inside you
after we have made love.

In bed and asleep, your eyelids
are all that covers you.

Don't pursue the fear,
don't say always, don't say never.
Give the world the liberty
to make its own way.

The space-time of trees is inside you
after we have made love.

Pleasure bathes you
as a tear does the eye.

Don't pursue the fear,
don't say always, don't say never.
Give the world the liberty
to make its own way.

The space-time of trees is inside you
after we have made love.

Haiku

Gau epela eta
ihintza azalean.
Bi gorputz ohantzean.

Haiku

Two naked bodies
in bed. The night's been mild, but
there's dew on their skin.

Gauza perfektuak

Oinentzat mesede izan arren, zapatentzat
sandaliek eskeletoen antza dute.
Olibondoak bi mila urte betetzen ditu
baina ez da ezertaz gogoratzen.

Gauza perfektuek ikara sortzen didate.
Ez ditut atsegin.
Nire letra okerra da, pausua okerragoa,
egin ahalak egin.

Things That Are Perfect

Though a favor to the feet, to the shoes
the sandals are bare skeletons.

An olive tree lives two thousand years
but tends to remember nothing.

Things that are perfect sow terror in me.
I don't like them.

My handwriting's skewed, my gait more so,
doing my best.

Ez da egia

Ez da egia. Ez naiz aldatu.
Nire ametsetan
hogei urte duzu beti.

It Isn't True

It's not true. I haven't changed.
In my dreams
you are twenty, always.

Four / *Lau*

Where to gather them in
the very person's
thousands of pieces

GEORGE SEFERIS

Bidaztia sorterriaz mintzo da

Betiko aberri galduaren
oroimen urruna. Ez dakigu
noiz galdu genuen: atzo ala bihar.

SOPHIA DE MELLO

Gure desertuan ez da harearik.
Metalezko hesia zeharkatu eta
autopistan futbolean jolasten duten
mutil koxkorrak badira.

Gure itsasoan ez da urik.
Mila zaldi urdin ziren uhinak.
Mila soldadurekin batera
eraman zituzten behin.

Gure desertuan ez da harearik.
Baina bada harresi erraldoia,
ezin ikusi dugun arren, hurretik,
oso hurretik inguratu gaituena.

Gure itsasoan ez da urik,
ez eta iraganaren uberarik.
Etorkizunak hondartzan dautza
malkoz eta ispilu hautsiez izorra.

Gure desertuan ez da urik.
Gure itsasoan ez da harearik.

The Traveler Speaks
of His Birthplace

> The perennial distant memory
> of the lost homeland. We don't know
> when we lost it: yesterday or tomorrow.
>
> SOPHIA DE MELLO

In our desert there is no sand.
There are growing boys
who cross the steel barriers and
play soccer on the thruway.

There is no water in our sea.
The waves were a thousand blue horses.
Once, with a thousand soldiers
they were carried away.

In our desert there is no sand.
But there's a giant wall of stone
which, though we can't see it,
has encircled us; closed in, close.

There is no water in our sea,
or any wake from the past.
Our futures recline on the beach,
big with tears and broken mirrors.

There is no water in our desert.
There is no sand in our sea.

Amesgaiztoa

Haurrekin amets egin dut gaur ere,
gerrako haurrekin.
Automobil batean zihoazen
muga zeharkatzeko asmoz, nagusirik gabe,
bakarrik, gidatzen ere doi-doi zekitela.
Gurasoek, etsiturik,
nahiago zuten haurrak auto-istripuz hiltzea
egunero bonbek urratzen duten hirian baino.
Ihesi zihoazen, halabeharrak utzitako
azken aukera profitatu nahian.

Esnatzeko eginahalak egin, baina
behin eta berriz hondoratzen nintzen amesgaizto hartan.
Beti amets bera.

Haurrekin egin dut amets. Gerrako haurrekin.
Neu ere haurra nintzen. Eta ihes egiten genuen,
mugarantz, kantari:
"Nora goaz? Ez dakit!
Nora goaz? Gu pozik!"

Bad Dream

I dreamt about children today, too,
the children of war.
They were going along in a car
hoping to cross the border, without any grown-ups,
alone, when they just barely knew how to drive.
Their parents, having despaired,
preferred their children to die on the highway
than in the city the bombs daily ripped apart.
They were running away, longing to take advantage
of the last chance their fate had left them.

Making every effort to wake up, but
time and again I sank down once more into that bad dream.
Always the same dream.

It was children I dreamt about. The children of war.
I was a child, too. And we were running away
toward the border, singing:
"Where are we going? I don't know!
Where are we going? Glad to go!"

Bidaia kaiera: Bhutan

Ahiturik iritsi dira turistak bordara.
Malkartsua izan da mendi arteko bide luzea.
Afari beroa paratu die etxeko nagusiak.
Leihoan ilargi betea, Himalaiako gailur zuriak.

Turistetako batek besteari:
"Oraindik ez dute jakingo menturaz
gizakia ilargian egon denik ere".
Etxeko nagusiari kontatu dio konkista.

Pentsakor jarri da bhutandarra. Ez du, ordea,
harridura eta miresmen keinurik adierazi.

Apal ihardetsi die begibitartea zimurtuz:
"Eta zenbat sherpa behar izan zituzten
ura hara goraino eramateko?"

Travel Notes: Bhutan

The tourists reached the shanty exhausted.
The long road through the mountains had been rugged.
The householder set out a hot supper for them all.
The full moon in the window, the white Himalayan peaks.

One of the tourists to another:
"It could be they don't even know yet
a man has been on the moon."
He told the householder of the conquest.

The Bhutanese became thoughtful. He did not, however,
show any sign of surprise or marveling.

He answered them mildly, wrinkling his brow:
"And how many sherpas did it take them
to get their water all the way up there?"

Memoria historikoa

Londres. Brixton auzoa. Eskuot batean hiru japoniar.
Afaria egin dugu. Bihar hegaldia daukat Bilbora.
Te beroaz Bigarren Mundu Gerra hizpide.
Japoniako zaharrek horri buruz ez dute ezer esaten,
kontatu du batek. Are gehiago, eskola-liburuetan
ez da gerrari buruz ia aipamenik agertzen.
Gutxi gorabehera, esaldi bakar hau:
"Bigarren Mundu Gerra
1942-1945 urteetan gertatu zen eta
Hiroshima eta Nagasakiko bonbekin amaitu".

Hegaldian noa Bilbora.
Txiki-txikiak dira hemendik Bizkaiko etxeak.

Historical Memory

London. Brixton. Three Japanese in a squat.
We've had supper. Tomorrow I fly to Bilbao.
Over hot tea, speaking of the Second World War:
The old people of Japan tell nothing about it,
one says. What's more, in the schoolbooks
there's nearly no mention at all of the war.
Or, more or less, this lone sentence:
"The Second World War
took place between 1942 and 1945 and
ended with the bombs at Nagasaki and Hiroshima."

Now on the flight to Bilbao.
The houses of Vizcaya are minute from here.

Sasiakazia

Martxoko arratsaldea hotz.
Lorazainek ongi burutu zuten lana.
Kimatu zituzten akaziak,
bildu adabakiak.

Zuhaitz elbarrituen artetik oinez.
Aluminiozko hodeiak.
Materia beltza eskanerrean.

Duela gutxi arte adarrak loturik zeuden,
pensatu dut nik.
Dagoeneko ez dakizu ni maitatzen, pensatu duzu zuk.

Errua ez da inoiz batena bakarrik izaten.

Martxoko arratsaldea hotz.
Negua da, ez gaitu utzi nahi.

False Acacia

March afternoon and cold.
The gardeners did a good job of work.
They pruned the acacias,
raked up the branches.

On foot through the crippled trees.
Clouds aluminum.
Black matter on the scanner.

Until just a moment ago, the branches had been attached,
I thought.
Already you haven't a clue how to love me, you thought.

The fault is never the fault of one person alone.

March afternoon and cold.
It's winter, it refuses to leave us.

Animalien hizkuntza

Italiako ipuin zaharretan ageri da nola aukeratzen zuten aita santua garai batean. Ipuinetan jasotzen denez, aita santua hil eta ondoko egunetan, jendez gainezka egoten zen San Petri plaza eta bertara uso zuri bat botatzen zuten. Usoa noren gainean pausa, horixe izango zen aita santua aurrerantzean. Baita munduko pertsonarik txiroena izanda ere, gizon ala emakume, usoak aukeratuko zuen aita santu berria. Aukeraketa, beraz, ez zen gaur egunekoa bezain korapilatsua. Atsegin dut txorien hizkuntza dakien mutikoaren elezaharra. Han hemenka kontatzen da ipuina, hizkuntza eta tradizio askotan. Batzuetan, ipuineko protagonistak txorien hizkuntza ez bakarrik, animalia guztiena daki, zakurrena, tripi-trapuena, izurdeena eta haiekin hitz egiten du. Ipuinak, gutxi gorabehera honelaxe dio: goiz batean, basotik bueltan, mutikoak aitari kontatuko dio txoriek esan diotela bihar edo etzi belaunikatu egingo dela aita semearen aurrean. Aitak gogor hartuko du mutila, denbora alferrik galdu duela esango dio semeari, lan egin beharrean txorien kantua entzuten eman dituelako egunak. Baina batez ere ez dio onartuko harrokeria, nolatan jarriko da aita ahuspez semearen aurrean. Eta etxetik botako du mutila, haserre bizian. Etxerik eta dirurik gabe, mutikoak hutsetik hasi beharko du. Eta horrela, aldian aldian txoriei entzunaz aita santu bihurtuko da azkenean mutila, aitaren damurako. Etxeko sukaldean ez da mundua ikusten.

The Language of the Animals

Among the old folktales of Italy
is the story of how at one time
they used to choose the pope.
As the taletellers had it,
in the days following a pope's death
St. Peter's Square would overflow
with people,
and they'd fling
a white dove
into the air.

Whoever the dove alighted on
would be pope thenceforward.
Even the poorest person on earth,
man or woman,
it was the dove that chose
the new pope. And so
the process of choosing
was not as complex
as it is nowadays.

I love the old story of the little boy
who knew the language of the birds,
you hear the tale here and there
all over. Sometimes he knows
not only the birds' language
but those of all the animals,
the dog's, the *tripi-trapu's*,
the wild boar's,
and he talks with all of them.

The tale, more or less,
the tale goes like this:

One morning, just back from the woods,
the little boy will tell his father
what the birds have said:
tomorrow, or the next day,
the father will kneel before his son.

The father will rebuke the boy:
he's been wasting his time,
listening to birdsong when he should
have been working,
the father will say,
and least of all will he accept
the brazen arrogance whereby
he is to prostrate himself
at his son's feet.

And he'll throw the boy out of the house in a fury.

With neither money nor home, the boy
will have to start over from scratch.
And in that very way,
slowly but surely, listening to the birds,
the boy will finally become pope,
to his father's remorse.

You don't see the world
from the kitchen of your house.

Hizkuntza bat

2004 ko urte berri egunean

Hizkuntza batek ez daki
onaren eta txarraren berri.
Hori gizakion kontua da.
Hizkuntza bat itzalaren antzekoa da.
Ukabila altxatuz gero
hark ere altxatu egingo du,
ihesi bazoaz, hark ere
zure atzetik egingo du ihes.

Hizkuntzak ez daki
egiaren ala gezurraren berri.
Hori gizakion kontua da.
Hizkuntza batek ez du hormarik eraikitzen,
kolorez pintatzen ditu.
hizkuntzak ez du inor hiltzen,
batu egiten gaitu.

Baina, hori bai, hizkuntza bat,
hizkuntza bat hil egiten da.

A Language

A language gets no word
of good and evil.
That is the business of us humans.
A language is like a shadow.
If you raise a fist,
it will raise one too.
If you run away, it too
will flee, right behind you.

A language gets no word
of truth or falsehood.
That is the business of us humans.
A language builds no walls,
it paints them in colors.
A language kills no one,
it brings us together.

But one thing to know about a language,
a language does die.

Hodeiak

Ihesi doaz hodeiak. Neguko
eguzkiaren usaina maindireek.
Goiz da oraindik.

Clouds

The clouds fly fleeing: winter
sheets, with their smell of the sun
in winter. It is still early.

Five / Bost

Words dry and riderless,
The indefatigable hoof-taps.

SYLVIA PLATH

Ezin esan

Ezin da esan Libertatea, ezin da esan Berdintasuna,
ezin da esan Anaitasuna, ezin esan.
Ez zuhaitz ez erreka ez bihotz.
Ahaztu egin da antzinako legea.

Uholak eraman du hitzen eta gauzen arteko zubia.
Ezin zaio esan tiranoak erabaki irizten dionari heriotz.
Ezin da esan norbait falta dugunean,
oroitzapen txikienak odolusten gaituenean.

Inperfektua da hizkuntza, higatu egin dira zeinuak
errotarri zaharrak bezala, ibiliaren ibiliz. Horregatik,

ezin da esan Maitasuna, ezin da esan Edertasuna,
ezin da esan Elkartasuna, ezin esan.
Ez zuhaitz ez erreka ez bihotz.
Ahaztu egin da antzinako legea.

Alabaina "ene maitea" zure ahotik entzutean
aitor dut zirrara eragiten didala,
dela egia, dela gezurra.

No Saying

No saying Liberty, no saying Equality,
no saying Fraternity—can't say it.
Not tree not stream not heart.
The ancienter law has been forgotten.

The flood's taken out the bridge from words to things.
Can't call what a tyrant thinks to decide death.
No saying when we're longing for somebody's presence,
when the smallest reminder empties the blood from a vein.

The language is unperfected, the signs worn down
as old millstones—the action of action. That's how come

no saying Love, no saying Beauty,
no saying Solidarity—can't say it.
Not tree not stream not heart.
The ancienter law has been forgotten.

Though when I've heard "my love" from your mouth,
I confess it has thrilled my being—
whether it's true or if a lie.

Bada beldur bat

Bada beldur bat abisurik gabe eta erabat hartzen gaituena,
otsaileko albatrosak itsaslabarretan bezala

gure gogoan pausatzen da,
dena ospel, dena uzkur, dena ahul bilakatuz.

Berehala etxera deitzera behartzen gaitu,
ahots ezaguna entzun eta lasaitzeko.

Eta, tamalez, aldika beldur hori
gaizto izaten da eta zehatz,

eta haize berdeak ekaitza halatsu
iragarri egiten du dohakabea.

Berri txarra aditu bezain laster hurbildu ginen ospitalera.
Osabak besoarekin inguratu eta alboratu egin ninduen.

Belarrira egiten zidan hitz eta nik bere eskua ikusten nuen soilik.
Txalupan mozoloak harrapatzeko gauza zen esku kakotu hura.

"Bizitzan gauza batzuk onartu egin behar dira.
Honek ez du batere itxura onik. Ausart izan behar duzu".

Inoiz ez naiz hain bakarrik sentitu.

There's a Fear

There's one fear that takes us whole and without warning.
Like an albatross in February over the sea cliffs,

it hangs in the mind,
turning everything frostbitten, shriveled, weak.

It makes us call home as quick as we can,
to hear the known voice and to calm down.

And sometimes—worse—the fear
goes bad and exact

and, as a green wind announces a storm,
foretells a misfortune.

As soon as we heard the bad news, we left for the hospital.
My uncle took me in his arms and drew me aside,

speaking right in my ear. I could see only his hand.
That hooked hand equal to catching little owls on the boat.

"Some things in life we just have to accept.
This doesn't look good at all. You have to be brave."

I've never felt so alone.

Gadda

Arauzko nobelarik behinena egitea zuen helburu
Carlo Emilio Gadda idazleak.
Ez zuen inoiz proiektua bukatzerik erdiesten.
Luzaroan izaten zen gogoeta egiten
eta esaldiak moldatzen
balizko nobela bukatu nahian.
Baina ez zuen inoiz lortzen.

Asmo horri amore ematen zionean bakarrik
argitaratzen zituen liburuak.
Bukatu gabeko kontakizunak ziren,
halabeharrez.

Izan ere, zatietan datza
errealitatearen muina.

Gadda

To write the one great novel of manners was the goal
of Carlo Emilio Gadda.
He never managed to complete the project.
Over ages he was contemplating it
and shaping sentences
in his longing to finish the hypothetical novel.
But he never achieved that.

Only when he gave in to that close-held longing
did he publish his books.
They were tales without ends,
by necessity.

i.e., reality's bone marrow
resides in its pieces.

Igogailua

Arreba eta biok
ospitalera itzuli gara hilabete geroago.
Eraikinean sartu ahala
urduri begiratu dugu hara eta hona,
haurrek plastikozko poltsetan eramaten dituzten
arrain gorriek bezala.
Ezkerrean, ebakuntzaren zain izan ginen gela.
Bertan igaro genuen azken gaua
umea espero zuen familiarekin batera.
Korridorearen bukaeran, igogailua.
Bi hilabetez eta egunean bitan
igotzen ginen bosgarren pisura,
zainketa berezien gelara,
egunero zer aurkituko,
berri onik noiz entzungo.

Azken txostenak sinatu ostean
irtetear gaudelarik,
igogailura begiratu eta esan diot arrebari:
"Igoko al gara gora?
Agian oraindik hantxe dago gure zain, ohean".

Begirakunea egin dit arrebak.
Urtsuak ditu begiak, txikiak
mendiko marrubien pareko.

The Elevator

My sister and I
went back to the hospital a month later.

As soon as we entered the building
we looked nervously here and there,
like the red fish
children carry home in plastic bags.

On the left, the pre-op waiting room.
There we spent the last night
with the family awaiting the birth
of their first child.

At the end of the corridor, the elevator.
For two months twice a day
we went up to the fifth floor,
to the intensive-care room,
hanging daily on what we'd find,
when we'd hear some good news.

After signing the last document
as we were about to leave,
after a look at the elevator
I say to my sister,
"Should we go up?
Maybe he's still there in bed
waiting for us."

My sister looks at me,
her eyes wet with tears
and as small as those
wild strawberries.

Arrain-ontzia

Arrain-ontziko arrain gorriek ez dakite
—bira eta bira—
badirela ibaietan bizi diren arrainak.

Ez dakite,
—bira eta bira—
itsasoa badenik ere.

Arrainontziko arrain gorriek ez dakite
—bira eta bira—
haiei begira gaudela, zain.

The Fishbowl

The red fish in the fishbowl don't know
—*bira eta bira,* circling round and around—
there are fish who live in the rivers.

They don't know—*bira eta bira,*
circling round and around—
there are any at all in the sea.

The red fish in the fishbowl don't know
—*bira eta bira,* circling round and around—
we are here waiting, looking to them.

Six / Sei

St. Jude and St. Simon,
summer had gone
and winter has come.

GABRIEL ARESTI

Aresti-Duchamp xake partida

ARESTI: Hire txanda, Marcel.

DUCHAMP: Ez zagok presarik.
Xakea marraztea bezala duk.
Buruan marrazten dituk mugimenduak
eta gero taulan.
Onena duk xake-taula ez dela kuadro bat,
behin bukatu eta hilik geratzen dena.
Bizia duk, Calder bat bezalakoa.
Ez zagok presarik. Mugimendu on batek,
lan on batek bezala,
bere denbora eskatzen dik.

ARESTI: Halako zerbait gertatu zitzaioan
margolari txinatar hari ere.
Enperadoreak karramarro baten marrazkia eskatu
ziolarik, margolariak jauregia eta
hamabi zerbitzari galdegin zizkioan trukean.
Eta bost urteko epea.
Bost urte igarota artean hasi gabe zegoelako
beste bost urteko epea eskatu zioan
enperadoreari. Hark eman.
Azkenik, pintzela hartu eta instant batean
marraztu zian karramarroa,
denik eta karramarrorik perfektuena.

(Duchampek zupada eman dio puruari eta dorrea jan.)

DUCHAMP: Dena den, aukera guztiak zitian
besoa moztu edo urkamendian bukatzeko.

The Aresti-Duchamp Chess Game

ARESTI: Your turn, Marcel.

DUCHAMP: No hurry, my friend.
    Chess works like drawing.
    You sketch the moves in your mind
    and then on the board.
    The best thing is, a chessboard's no canvas,
    dead and done when it's done.
    This, it's alive, like a Calder.
    You've no need to rush. Your good move,
    your good piece of work,
    takes exactly its own sweet time.

ARESTI: Something like that happened
    to that Chinese painter who,
    when the Emperor requested
    a picture of a crab, asked for a palace
    and twelve servants in return.
    And five years' time.
    And since through those five years
    he started on nothing,
    he asked for another five years,
    by the Emperor's grace. Granted.
    At the very end, he took up his brush
    and in an instant painted the Emperor his crab,
    the most perfect of all crabs, mind you.

(Duchamp takes a long pull on his cigar, along with a rook.)

DUCHAMP: Anyhow, he had every chance
    of losing an arm, or winding up hanged.

Lana ez bukatzea zen litekeena.
Atera kontuak, neuk ere hamar urte
igaro nitian "Beira handia" egiten.
Aspaldi utzi nioan pintatzeari,
hogeita bost urte besterik ez nituela.
Ezertxo ere egiten ez nuela uste zitean.
Neurri batean egia zuan, bizitza bilakatu zuan
garai batean nire artelanik behinena.
Baina tarteka ekiten nioan proiektu eskerga horri.
Zorigaitzaren kontuak, azkenik
bukatu gabe zegoela saldu nian,
diru gabe eta gogaiturik.

ARESTI: Zakurrek egiten ditek dantza diruagatik.

DUCHAMP: Gasturik ezean ez duk dirurik behar.
Zenbat eta gauza gehiago nahi
orduan eta zor gehiago.
Ezer gutxi izatea duk onena.

(Arestik bi pieza jan dizkio mugimendu bakar batean.)

ARESTI: Ezer gabe geratuko haiz
horrela jokatzen baduk.
Ez duk batere defentsa onik.

DUCHAMP: Soldaduzka ez egitearren izango duk.

ARESTI: Nik neuk ere ez nian luzaroan egin.
Soldaduei idazten eta nagusiei
ingelesa irakasten niean.
Etxetik arrabete bidera.

Not getting the work done at all was most likely.
If you added it up, I spent ten years myself
making *Large Glass*.
I'd long since given up painting,
only twenty-five years old.
They thought I was doing exactly nothing.
To a degree it was true, life
became my one and only artwork, at one time.
But in between times I was taking up that vast project.
Matter of bad luck, finally,
you know, I sold it unfinished,
depressed and no money.

ARESTI: Dogs do the dance for money.

DUCHAMP: Keep from spending it, you don't need money.
   The more things you crave
   the greater your debt.
   Best thing of all is having little enough.

(Aresti takes two men in a single move.)

ARESTI: You'll be left with nothing
   if that's how you play it.
   Not a good defense you've got there.

DUCHAMP: That's because I never did do time in the army.

ARESTI: I wasn't in long myself.
   Writing to the soldiers and
   teaching English to the brass,
   a stone's throw from home.

DUCHAMP: Abokatuak eta medikuak
hobe moldatzen zituan gurean.
Eta baita arte langileak ere.
Grabatuak egiten zitian aitonak.
Neu ere grabatugilea nintzela
agindu niean erroldakoei.
Jakina, ez nian ideiarik.
Hala ere, ganbara miatu,
aitonaren xafla zaharrak hartu
eta horrelaxe agertu ninduan tribunalera.
Oso-osorik sinetsi zitean.

ARESTI: Gaztetan ere plazagizon.

DUCHAMP: Ez dago arterik entzulerik gabe.
Picasso eta Metzinger zatozkidak burura.
Kubismoa famako egin aurretik
Metzinger zegoan ahominean.
Azaldu egiten zian hark kubismoa.
Gero konturatu gintuan ez zela azalpenik behar.
Picasso agertu eta bandera bilakatu zuan berehala.
Jendeak ez zian besterik nahi.
Metzinger gaixoa ahaztu egin zitean.

ARESTI: Poesiak ere ez dik esplikaziorik behar.
Lizardi konprenitu egiten duk,
heldu egiten duk.
Isiltasunak inguratzen dik hitza.
Isiltasun horretan zabaldu behar dituk leihoak.
Pentsa, Amazoniako indiarrek
zuloak zabaltzen ditiztek oihanean.
Lurra landatu eta urte beteren buruan
berriz luzatzen dituk zuhaitzak.
Oihanean zuloak egin behar ditiztek hitzek.

DUCHAMP: The lawyers and doctors
   got along better in ours.
   And artisans, too.
   My grandfather did engravings.
   When I went to the recruiting station
   I told them I was an engraver as well.
   Of course, I didn't have a clue.
   But I scoured the attic,
   took my granddad's old plates
   and showed them to the warrant officers.
   They believed me down to the ground.

ARESTI: Looking alive as a young fellow, too.

DUCHAMP: There's no art without a listener.
   Picasso and Metzinger spring to mind, no?
   Before Cubism became famous
   Metzinger was on everyone's tongue.
   He was the one talking up Cubism.
   Later we realized no one needed telling.
   Picasso comes along, becomes the talisman.
   People didn't want anything else.
   They forgot all about poor old Metzinger.

ARESTI: Now, poetry needs no explanation whatever.
   We all understand Lizardi,
   we get him.
   Silence surrounds every word.
   In that silence, you've got to open the windows.
   Think of it, the Indians of the Amazon
   break holes through the rain forest.
   They work the land and at the end of a year
   the trees are up again.
   Words have to break holes through the jungle.

Soilik behar beharrezkoak diren zuloak,
oihan guztia biluztu gabe.
Baina arrazoi duk,
idazle batentzat inportanteena
irakurria izatea duk.

(Duchampek pieza mugitu du pentsakor.)

DUCHAMP: Zer botatzen duk gehien faltan?

ARESTI: Etxekoak, lagunak, oinak lurrean izatea.
Beti flotean ibili behar honek
nekatzen naik. Nork esango
hilondoan flotatzen egongo ginela denok
hodeiak bezala, lantzean lantzean
norbaitekin elkartuz, dela erromatarra,
dela bikingoen garaikoa,
dela Etxeberri Sarakoa.
Onena elkarrizketak dituk,
hainbeste jenderekin gertatzea.

DUCHAMP: Nik ez nian honelakorik espero.
Infernuko ideiak ere tentatu egiten nindian.
Halako errepublika libre bat izateak,
inolako araurik gabea.
Nik uste Cravanek ere
halako zerbait espero zuela
Mexikon desagertu zelarik.
Lagun guztiei deitu, portuan agurtu
eta txalupa batean alde egin zian bakarrik,
ur handietara.
Oraindik ez diat harekin topo egin.

Only the absolutely necessary holes,
without stripping the whole forest.
But you're right,
the most important thing for a writer
is being read.

(Duchamp moves a piece, pensive.)

DUCHAMP: What is it you miss most, yourself?

ARESTI: The people at home, friends, having my feet on the ground.
    This business of having always to keep floating
    exhausts me. Who'd have predicted
    after death we'd be incessantly floating,
    like clouds, every so often getting together
    with someone, maybe a Roman,
    maybe someone from the age of the Vikings,
    or Etxeberri of Sara perhaps.
    What's best are the conversations,
    time with so many people.

DUCHAMP: I didn't expect anything of the kind.
    The idea of Hell had its temptations.
    Its being a free republic that way,
    with no regulations of any kind.
    I think Cravan, too,
    hoped for something like that
    when he disappeared in Mexico.
    Calling all his friends, good-byes at the port,
    and going off alone in a skiff,
    off to his high seas.
    No one's met up with him since.

ARESTI: Bilbon izan nahiko nikek nik,
   berriro ibaian bainatu
   eta Abadiñoko harriak ikusi,
   dozena bat antigualeko harri
   biribilean jarririk, batzarrak egiteko.

DUCHAMP: Ez zituan ba margolariak batzeko izango?

ARESTI: Ez, gizona.

DUCHAMP: Idazleak?

ARESTI: Ezta ere. Baina gogoan diat
   aurrekoan Oihenartek eta Mirandek
   nortasun txartelak trukatu zituztela
   literatur kongresu batean.
   Mirandek Oihenarten argazkia paparrean,
   Oihenartek Miranderena.
   Barregarria izan zuan.

(Arestik patrikatik errekarri txiki bat atera du.)

ARESTI: Harriak botatzen ditiat faltan.

DUCHAMP: Hik harriak eta nik beira.
   Ez diagu bikote txarra egiten.
   Beirak ezkutukoa uzten dik agerian,
   beirazkoak dituk leihoak,
   beirazkoak godaletak,
   beirazkoak hareazko erlojuak.

(Harrizko dorrea mugitzeko keinua egin du Arestik.)

ARESTI: Ez zaiguk jokatzeko pieza asko geratzen . . .

ARESTI: I'd rather be in Bilbao,
   swimming in the river again,
   rather see the stones of Abadiño,
   a dozen ancient stones
   set in a circle, for the convocations.

DUCHAMP: These were painters getting together?

ARESTI: No sirree.

DUCHAMP: Writers?

ARESTI: Not so. But you've got me recalling
   when two writers once swapped centuries
   at a literary congress: Oihenart
   with Mirande's photo ID
   on his shirtfront,
   Mirande with Oihenart's.
   You can believe it was funny.

(Aresti takes a small, stream-rounded pebble from a pocket.)

ARESTI: I miss the stones.

DUCHAMP: You miss the stones, I miss the glass.
   We wouldn't make a bad pair.
   Glass lets what's hidden show,
   windows are glass,
   as are your goblets,
   your hourglasses.

(Aresti gestures him to move the stone castle.)

ARESTI: Not many pieces left to play here . . .

DUCHAMP: Nik ez diat gogoko partidak bukatzea.
Badakik liburu bat idatzi nuela
oso gutxitan gertatzen den
xake mugimendu bati buruz.
Mugimendu horretan
ezin ziok batek besteari irabazi.
Oso gutxitan gertatzen duk;
gu biok elkar topatzeko bezain
aukera gutxi zaudek,
planeta guztiak lerroan jartzea bezain.
Onena beste kasualitate baterako
ixtea izango duk.
Mendeak eta mendeak ditiagu
aurretik, Gabriel.

ARESTI: Ados.

(Duchampek eskua luzatu dio Arestiri.)

DUCHAMP: Plazer bat izan duk.

ARESTI: Laster arte.

> *(Trapezistak balira bezala elkarri tira egin eta bata alde
> batera eta bestea bestera joan dira, geldo, hodeien gisara.)*

DUCHAMP: I don't like the games to end, you know.
 You heard I wrote a book
 about a chess move
 that comes up only very rarely.
 With that move, it's impossible
 for players to beat each other.
 Happens only very seldom,
 about as often as the chances
 of the two of us meeting up,
 or all your planets aligning.
 Might be best if we left it
 for another coincidence.
 We've got centuries and centuries
 ahead of us, Gabriel.

ARESTI: Agreed.

(Duchamp holds out his hand, to shake on it.)

DUCHAMP: It's been a pleasure.

ARESTI: Be seeing you soon.

  (As if they were trapeze artists, they take one another's hand
  and—slowly—cross over, one one way, the other the other,
  in the manner of clouds.)

Seven / Zazpi

I asked the professors who teach the meaning of life to
    tell me what is happiness.
And I went to famous executives who boss the work of
    thousands of men.
They all shook their heads and gave me a smile as though
    I was trying to fool with them
And then one Sunday afternoon I wandered out along
    the Desplaines river
And I saw a crowd of Hungarians under the trees with
    their women and children and a keg of beer and
    an accordion.

CARL SANDBURG

Ez eman hautatzeko

Ez eman hautatzeko
Itsasoa eta Lehorraren artean.
Gustura bizi naiz itsaslabarrean,
Haizeak mugitzen duen zinta beltz honetan,
Gizandi erratu bati eroritako ile luze honetan.

Itsasoarena maite dut batez ere bihotza.
Inozoa, haur handi batena bezain.
Orain temoso, orain ezinezko paisaiak
Marrazten.
Lehorrarena berriz
Esku handi horiek ditut gogokoen.

Ez eman hautatzeko
Itsasoa eta Lehorraren artean.
Badakit hari fin bat dela nire bizilekua,
Baina Itsasoarekin bakarrik galduko nintzateke,
Lehorrarekin ito.

Ez eman hautatzeko. Hemen geratuko naiz.
Olatu berde eta mendi urdinen artean.

Don't Make It a Choice

Don't make me choose
Between the Sea and Dry Land.
I relish living on the edge of the sea cliff,
On this black ribbon the wind waves,
On this long hair fallen from an errant giant.

Of the Sea I love especially its heart,
As idiotic as a great child's.
Now headstrong, wayward, now drawing
Impossible landscapes.
Of Dry Land, however,
I most love those great hands.

Don't make me choose
Between the Sea and Dry Land.
I know my residence is a fine line of thread,
But I'd be lost with only the Sea,
Drown with Dry Land.

Don't make it a choice. I'm going to stay here.
Between the green waves and the blue mountains.

Urrezko eraztuna

Aitak itsasoan galdu zuen ezkontzako eraztuna. Marinel guztiek bezala, kendu egiten zuen hatzetik eta lepokoan jarri, sarea largatzean hatza gal ez zezan.

Handik marea batzuetara izebak, legatz batzuk garbitzen ari zelarik, urrezko eraztun bat aurkitu zuen arrainetako baten sabelean.

Eraztuna garbitu, eta grabatuta zituen letra eta zenbakiei jarri zien arreta. Gezurra zirudien arren, gurasoen ezkontza eguna ematen zuten aditzera datak eta inizialek.

Itxura guztien arabera, aitak berak harrapatu zuen eraztuna jan zion legatz hura. Itsasorik zabalenean.

Udako gau bareak barruko haizea dakar eta oroitzapenak.

Kasualitateak orbita zabal-zabaleko planetak direla otu zait zeruari begira.

Behin edo behin ageri dira bakarrik.

Eraztunarena kasualitate handiegia da. Baina ez du axola. Inportanteena orain hauxe da: urte askoan eraztunaren istorio hori sinesgarri egin zitzaiela gure haur adimen txikiei.

Gauez, itsasoak legatz baten distira du.
Izarrek salto egiten dute ezkaten antzera.

The Gold Ring

Father lost his wedding ring in the ocean once. Like all the trawl-ermen, he'd take it from his finger to put on a neck chain, not to lose the finger as the net went out.

Several tides after that, our aunt, while cleaning some hake, found a gold ring in the belly of one of the fish.

Once she'd washed it off, she examined the letters and numbers engraved inside. Though it couldn't be true, the date and the initials were those of our parents' wedding.

By all appearances, Father himself had caught the hake that had swallowed the ring. In all of the wide blue sea.

Peaceable summer nights bring the inland wind, and the memories.

I look at the sky, and it dawns that coincidences are the planets with the amplest orbits.

Only every so often have they come round.

The ring's is far too great a coincidence. It would have been lost and found in that same stone sink. But that doesn't matter. What's most important now is this: for years and years, the story of the ring was entirely believable to our small, children's intelligence.

Nights, the ocean has the shimmer of hake.
The stars go leaping around like the scales.

Oroimen ariketa

"Ez dut negarrez aritzea besterik
esku-ahurrak desegin artean"
idatzi nuela daukat gogoan.

Carver-ek hil baino hilabete bat lehenago
erosketetako papertxoan idatzi zuena ere
badatorkit: "Gurina, arrautzak, txokolatea . . .

Antartidara joan ala Australiara?"
Uholak dakartzan adar eta plastikozko
ontziak dira egun oroitzapenak.

Eta kalean galdu nuen lagunminaren
betarte zurbila ere badakarkit.
Bere irribarre konplizea.

"Ez dut negarrez aritzea besterik
esku-ahurrak desegin artean"
idatzi nuela daukat gogoan.

Gordean ditut halaber
neurria hartu nahia, aldatzeko ahalegina,
nire mamuekin irauteko premia,

eta denbora arretaz ehundu
begiekin, malkoekin, eskuekin,
itzalen luzapenak bizirik harrapa nazan.

Memory Exercise

"All that's left to do now is cry
till my hands come apart in my hands,"
I wrote, I'm remembering.

What Carver, a month before dying, wrote down
in a short shopping list
comes to mind: "Butter, eggs, chocolate . . .

Go to Antarctica—or else Australia?"
The branches and plastic containers
the flood brings are today's rememberings.

And the countenance of that loved one
I lost in the street: pale
as the flood presents it. That purely complicitous smile.

"All that's left to do now is cry
till my hands come apart in my hands,"
I wrote, I'm remembering.

I'm likewise secretly harboring
the urge to take stock, the desire to change,
a haste to keep on with my demon-phantoms

and carefully knit up the time
with my eyes, these tears, my hands,
so our shadows' lengthening shadow can take me alive.

Kukua

Aitzoli

Apirilaren hasieran entzun zuen aurrena kukua.
Urduri zebilelako beharbada,
kaosa ordenatzeko joera horrengatik beharbada,
kukuak zein notatan kantatzen zuen jakin nahi izan zuen.

Hurrengo arratsaldean, hantxe egon zen basoan zain,
diapasoia eskuan, kukuak noiz kantatuko.
Diapasoiak ez zioen gezurrik.
Si-sol ziren kukuaren notak.

Aurkikuntzak bazterrak astindu zituen.
Mundu guztiak frogatu nahi zuen benetan
nota horietan kantatzen ote zuen kukuak.
Baina neurketak ez zetozen bat.
Bakoitzak bere egia zuen.
Fa-re zirela zioen batek, Mi-do besteak.
Ez ziren ados jartzen.

Bitartean, kukuak kantari jarraitzen zuen basoan:
ez si-sol, ez fa-re, mi-do ezta ere.
Mila urte lehenago bezala,
kukuak kuku, kuku kantatzen zuen.

The Cuckoo

to Aitzol

He heard the first cuckoo at the beginning of April.
Because he'd been feeling on edge, maybe,
from an inclination to order the chaos, maybe,
he wanted to know which notes the cuckoo sang.

He sat waiting with his pitch pipe
next afternoon: when
would the cuckoo sing?
He finally achieved it:
the pitch pipe told no lies.
Si-sol were the cuckoo's notes.

The discovery shook the countryside.
Everyone wanted to prove whether truly those
were the notes that the cuckoo sang.
The measurements were not in harmony.
Each had his or her own truth.
One said it was *fa-re,* another *mi-do.*
No one managed to agree.

Meanwhile the cuckoo went on singing in the forest,
not *mi-do,* not *fa-re,* not *si-sol,* either.
As it had a thousand years before,
the cuckoo sang *cuccu, cuccu.*

Aparte-apartean

Sei urterekin egin zuten lehen itsasoratzea aitak eta osabak,
eta patroitza Bustio baporean ikasi.
Gogorrak ziren garai hartako patroiak,

ekaitz egunetan ukabilak estutu eta zerura begira
"bizarrik badaukazu etorri hona!"
Jainkoari amenazu egiten zieten horietakoak.

Mutil koskorrak zirenean, igandeko mezetara
txandaka joan behar izaten zuten lau anai nagusiek,
traje bakarra baitzen etxean. Bata elizatik etorri,

trajea erantzi, besteari eman
eta horrela joaten ziren mezetara,
nor bere orduan, nor bere zapatez.

Umetan, aita itsasotik iristen zen egunean,
portuko morro luzeenean egoten ginen zain
mendebaldera begira. Hasieran

ezer ikusten ez bazen ere, laster
antzematen zuen gutariko batek hodeiertzean
puntu beltz bat, pixkanaka itsasontzi bilakatzen zena.

Ordu beteren buruan heltzen zen ontzia morrora,
eta bira egiten zuen gure aurrean portura sartzeko.
Aitak agur egiten zigun eskuaz.

Ontzia igaro orduko, ariniketan joaten ginen
atrakatu behar zuten tokira.
Aita ohean azkenetan zegoela ere

Way Off Over There

My father and uncle were six years old when they first
went out with the boats, and learned seamanship on the Bustio.
The captains of the time were tough,

on stormy days set to raise a fist and stare down God,
"If you've got a beard on your face, c'mon in!"
Ready to threaten Heaven, that kind.

When they were boys, the four oldest had to take turns
going to Mass: just the one suit in the house.
One would come back from church,

take the suit off, pass it on to the next
and that's how they went to Mass,
each at his own hour, each in his own shoes.

When we were kids, on the longest jetty in port
the day Dad came in from sea, we'd wait and wait
watching out to the west. Even if in the beginning

we all saw nothing at all, soon
someone glimpsed off there against the horizon-cloud
a black dot, which slowly turned into a boat on the sea.

At the end of an hour the boat reached the seawall
and wheeled before us to enter the port.
Dad waved his hand in greeting.

As the boat passed we'd race
to where they were about to moor it.
Even when Dad was in bed at the last,

gorazarre egiten zion bizitzari,
eguna bizi behar dela esaten zigun,
beti arduratuta ibiliz gero ihes dagiela bizitzak.

Eta agintzen zuen: Beti iparralderago
joan behar duzue, ez da sarea bota behar
arraina ziur dagoela dakizuen tokian,

aparte-apartean bilatu behar da,
daukazuenarekin konformatu gabe.
"Heriotzak ez du irabaziko"

idatzi zuen Dylan Thomasek,
baina nonoiz irabazten du,
eta halaxe amatatu zen aitaren bizitza ere,

mendebaldera eginez
hodeiertzean galtzen zen itsasontzia bezala,
uberan oroitzapenak marraztuz.

he was singing the praises of life,
saying the day has to be lived. The moment
you start to worry, life escapes you.

And invariably: Listen up, the bunch of you, you've got to
head farther north, the net doesn't have to go out
where you know for sure the fish are,

you've got to search way off over there,
not settle for what you have.
"Death shall have no dominion,"

wrote Dylan Thomas, but it wins
a dominion now and again,
and Dad's life ended that way, too,

heading way off to the west
a boat gotten lost on the clouds' edge,
sketching the reminders in its wake.

Notak paper solte batean

Gogoratu etxera luze gabe deitzea.
Kaina-bera luzeak mugitzen ikustea.
Neure burua hainbeste berriz ez zigortzea.
Azken trena galdu eta hurrena itxarotea.

Zauritutako eskuak errekan garbitzea.
Tristura gabe pozik ez dela jakitea.
Goizaren beirazko laztana muxuan sentitzea.
Deabruaren eskaintzak noizbehinka onartzea.

Agian dena aldatzen ahal da.
Agian nonbait biderik bada.

Gogoratu traba egiten dizun horretaz mintzatzea.
Ubarroiei begira isilik egotea.
Beldur eta zalantzei eskua luzatzea.
Norabiderik gabe bakarrik gidatzea.

Notes on a Loose Piece of Paper

Remember to call home before too long.
To see the long reeds when they are in motion.
Not to punish myself as much as that again.
To miss the last train and wait for the next.

To wash off your injured hands in the creek.
Know there is no happiness without sadness.
Feel the glass caress of morning in the kiss.
Accept what the Devil offers once in a while.

Perhaps everything can in fact change.
Perhaps there's any road at all somewhere.

Remember to tell what blocks you at every turn.
Not speak while watching the cormorants.
Hold out a hand to the doubts and fears.
Drive along alone without orientation.

Maiatza

Utzi begietara begiratzen.
Nola zauden jakin nahi dut.

RAINER W. FASSBINDER

Begira, sartu da maiatza,
Zabaldu du bere betazal urdina portuan.
Erdu, aspaldian ez dut zure berri izan,
Ikarati zabiltza, ito ditugun katakumeak bezala.
Erdu eta egingo dugu berba betiko kontuez,
Atsegin izatearen balioaz,
Zalantzekin moldatu beharraz,
Barruan ditugun zuloak nola bete.
Erdu, sentitu goiza aurpegian,
Goibel gaudenean dena irizten zaigu ospel,
Adoretsu gaudenean, atzera, papurtu egiten da mundua.
Denok gordetzen dugu betiko besteren alde ezkutu bat,
Dela sekretua, dela akatsa, dela keinua.
Erdu eta larrutuko ditugu irabazleak,
Zubitik jauzi egin geure buruaz barre.
Isilik begiratuko diegu portuko garabiei,
Elkarrekin isilik egotea baita
adiskidetasunaren frogarik behinena.
Erdu nirekin, herriz aldatu nahi dut,
Nire gorputz hau albo batera utzi
Eta maskor batean zurekin sartu,
Gure txikitasunarekin, mangolinoak bezala.
Erdu, zure zain nago,
Duela urtebete etendako istorioa jarraituko dugu,
Ibai ondoko urki zuriek uztai bat gehiago ez balute bezala.

May

Let me look at those eyes.
I want to know how you are.

RAINER W. FASSBINDER

Look. May has come in.
It's strewn those blue eyes all over the harbor.
Come, I haven't had word of you in ages.
You're constantly terrified,
Like the kittens we drowned when we were little.
Come and we'll talk over all of the old same things,
The value of being pleasant,
The need to adjust to the doubts,
How to fill the holes we've got inside us.
Come, feel the morning reaching your face,
Whenever we're saddened everything looks dark,
When we're heartened, again, the world crumbles.
Every one of us keeps forever someone else's hidden side,
If it's a secret, if a mistake, if a gesture.
Come and we'll flay the winners,
Laughing at our self leapt off the bridgeway.
We'll watch the cranes at work in the port in silence,
The gift for being together in silence being
The principal proof of friendship.
Come with me, I want to change nations,
Change towns. Leave this body aside
And go into a shell with you,
With our smallness, like sea snails.
Come, I'm waiting for you,
We'll continue the story that ended a year ago,
As if inside the white birches next to the river
Not a single additional ring had grown.

Afterword: Anus mundi

March 11, 2004

In 1941, the Germans proposed renaming Poland "Anus mundi," the asshole of the world. At that same time, the Polish writer Milosz was writing calm, serene poems, without putting on paper any of the destruction taking place in his country. And when he was asked the reason for that choice—when they took him to task over whether he wasn't perhaps fleeing responsibility, wasn't even perhaps looking the other way—he responded that he'd made the choice he had because he was unable to bear the reality, because it was impossible for him to put what had come to pass in Poland into a lyric. For him, words are always on the side of life, never on the side of death. Words resemble a body that even nearing death wants to stay alive; they cling to breath, until the very last moment. In Milosz's view, the calm, serene words that are spoken in bad times publicly declare on the side of life, and help a person set his house in order, even if the order resembles that of a child's room.

We need calm, serene words around here. Calm, serene words to solve our problems. Calm, serene words at a remove from the heated expoundings and surface readings, at a remove from vengeance. Calm, serene words to get to the bottom of the problems, and calm, serene words so that we as people will not be used. The Nazis called Poland "Anus mundi," the asshole of the world. We need calm, serene words so our entire world may not itself become the asshole of all creation.

Notes

"The Beech Tree" (p. 19)—Manuel Antonio Imaz of Altzo (1811–1919) was in fact not a poet but a *bertsolari* (I have heard the term translated as "troubadour," by someone who was probably not kidding), as was Pello Errota himself. Errota, though, composed in the spontaneously sung tradition, while Imaz set his verses in writing, to be disseminated as broadside pamphlets. And what Pello Errota says here is that Imaz was among the best of all poets of that kind.

Beneath the beech tree—today in fact five normal-sized belt-lengths around, beside a dirt road in the woods above the last house in Altzo (Gipuzkoa)—is a stone marker that says, in Euskara:

> Planted
> by Manuel Antonio Imaz,
> *bertsolari* born in Altzo,
> on the day he was married,
> 22nd of September 1836,
> so that the shadow
> of this changed beech
> might gather us together,
> his descendants and successors
> IX-22-97

"Mohammed" (p. 21)—In both earlier editions, the title of the poem on page 20 was "Mahmud." When the book came out in Spanish, Kirmen Uribe was horrified to learn that in Tangiers, where the poem's speaker is from, the name is never shortened in the way he had done there. He wanted to make sure to correct the error.

"Apples" (p. 49)—Beñat Etxepare, a pre-Counterreformation poet and cleric, was the author of *Lingua Vasconum Primitiae* (1545), the first book ever printed in Euskara. Etxepare's poetry took as its themes religion (since his religion leaned toward the Lutheran, one lone copy of the book survived destruction), love, sex, the language itself, and daily life. It was poetry that people knew by heart, Uribe told me. A pastor who wrote from his own "I" and was an optimist about the language, Etxepare originated a phrase that is continually cited and discussed to this day: "to bring Euskara into the plaza."

"The Aresti-Duchamp Chess Game" (p. 95)—Gabriel Aresti (1933–1975) was born in Bilbao, the Basque industrial city and steel town that, along with Barcelona, supported the rest of Spain during the Franco years. A leftist by conviction, Aresti began studying Euskara when he was eighteen, at a time when that, too, was a dangerous political act, and he published the first of his five books of poetry in 1960. His poems spoke to social subject matters—politics, immigration, industry, the struggle against Franco—from the viewpoint of an urban "I" that could at times be Walt Whitman's, and he brought Basque poetry out of a symbolist tradition into a new, urban realism. A vigorous participant in the movement to create Euskara Batua (Unified Basque), in 1967 Aresti founded the literary press Lur, which became a focal point for writers in the language in the 1960s and 1970s. He was a translator of Federico García Lorca, and of T. S. Eliot's "Four Quartets." Many of his poems have been set to music over the years, and of those a number have become traditional.

(page 99) Xabier Lizardi (1896–1933). One of the great renovators of poetry in Euskara. He absorbed and brought to Basque literature the impulse of European Vanguardism, to make a poetry that was coloristic, with a tinge of Modernism, and meant for the page. Lizardi's *Biotz begietan (The Eyes of the Heart)* was published in 1932. A contemporary of Federico García Lorca and the Catalan Salvador Espriu, Lizardi is thought to be the best of a generation of fine Basque poets whose lives or careers ended at the time of the Spanish Civil War. While two of them, Aitzol and Lauaxeta, were shot and one, Orixe, was exiled, Lizardi died, of tuberculosis, three years before the Fallangist uprising.

(page 101) A physician and writer from Sara (Sare), in the French Basque province of Labourd, Joanes Etxeberri (1668–1749) was a man of the Enlightenment, and forward-looking with regard to the language and its place in literature, education, and science. When I asked Uribe what Gabriel Aresti might have found if he could indeed have met up with Etxeberri, he said, "Clarity, an optimism regarding life."

(page 103) Jon Mirande (1925–1972)—A poet and writer controversial in the Basque Country. Born in Paris of parents from Labourd, Mirande did not learn Euskara until he was out of childhood, and he began publishing poems in it when he was twenty-five. His poetry was provocative in the Nitzschean mode and, as Uribe put it, relished its ironies. When Mirande was in his early thirties, he wrote a novel that has been called the Basque *Lolita:* as soon as it was finished, in 1959, *Haur besoetakoa (Godchild)* managed to alienate the greater part of the ur-Catholic Basque-nationalist literary world. (In this respect, for all that it dealt with pederasty, it was really more of a *Portnoy's Complaint.*) It wasn't until 1970 that the book was finally published, by Gabriel Aresti at Lur. By then, Mirande had settled in Brittany, begun studying Breton, and had become an adherent of Celtism, a movement stressing the kinship of all the Celtic languages and cultures. (Breton is a dialect of Gaelic.) At the same time, he turned to pantheism, and delved more deeply into Celtic mythology. In 1972, he spent time in a sanatarium in the Breton town of Chateaulin. He committed suicide, in Paris, on Christmas Eve of that year.

(page 103) Arnaud Oihenart (1592–1667). Historian and poet in the Baroque tradition, a creator of neologisms and new metrics, and of poems written entirely for the page. In a way, as Uribe put it, Oihenart's first language was poetry. Born in Soule, on the French side, Oihenart was a cultured bourgeois and a harsh critic of Etxepare's 1545 originary work. But nowadays, as Uribe said, "you understand Etxepare, but not Oihenart."

E.M.

Kirmen Uribe was born in 1970 in Ondarroa, Spain, where he currently lives and writes. His debut poetry collection, *Bitartean heldu eskutik (Meanwhile Take My Hand)*, won Spain's 2001 Premio de la Crítica, and has since been translated from the Basque original into Spanish, French, and English. He is also a newspaper columnist and children's book author, and has been a teacher, scriptwriter, lyricist, and multimedia and music collaborator. He is currently at work on a novel.

Elizabeth Macklin is the author of two books of poetry, *A Woman Kneeling in the Big City* (1992) and *You've Just Been Told* (2000). A recipient of a 1994 Guggenheim Fellowship in Poetry, the 1999 Amy Lowell Poetry Traveling Scholarship, and a 2005 PEN Translation Fund grant for *Meanwhile Take My Hand*, she is currently at work on poems for a third collection. She lives in New York City.

nn Sudmeier. It is set in
.......ing Center, and manufac-
tured by Versa Press on acid-free paper.